JOHN SINCLAIR

HIGHLAND
BUSES

AMBERLEY PUBLISHING

The quintessential MacBrayne service coach of the 1950s was the Park Royal bodied Maudslay Marathon, of which thirty were operated. Here FUS997, new in 1948, descends to the Corran Ferry in August 1962 to provide a summer connection to Acharacle, en route from Fort William to North Ballachulish, where it was garaged overnight. Two months later it was sold to Smith of Grantown, who operated it for another two and a half years, providing services to the skiers on Cairngorm.

Dedicated to my wife Ann and children Roz and Paul, who sat patiently in the car waiting for a 'unique' bus to appear at the perfect location to photograph it.

First published 2013

Amberley Publishing Plc
The Hill, Stroud
Gloucestershire, GL5 4EP

www.amberley-books.com

Copyright © John Sinclair, 2013

The right of John Sinclair to be identified as the Author of this work has been asserted in accordance with the Copyrights, Designs and Patents Act 1988.

ISBN: 978 1 4456 1473 1 (print)
ISBN: 978-1-4456-1479-3 (e-book)

British Library Cataloguing in Publication Data.
A catalogue record for this book is available from the British Library.

Typeset in 9.5pt on 12pt Celeste.
Typesetting by Amberley Publishing.
Printed in the UK.

Introduction

6 October 1961 was a memorable day for me. I had signed out of the cells at Thurso Police Station at 6 a.m. and walked up to the Highland Omnibuses depot to catch the staff bus out to the Dounreay nuclear reactor, where nearly forty buses would arrive from all over Caithness. Although I had been taking snaps of buses with a box camera since 1956, I had just bought a 35mm camera from a family friend and could now take coloured slides. I had hitch hiked up from my family home in Edinburgh, this being my usual form of transport. Where possible I stayed in youth hostels but there were none near Thurso, and I had discovered that provided one arrived after midnight, some police stations would offer very basic overnight accommodation.

This was a trusted and reliable formula that allowed me to travel around the country for nearly ten years, documenting information about and photographing buses. While I travelled mainly throughout Scotland, I had spent my earlier years in Yorkshire and often hitch hiked in the north of England and also southern Ireland. I had relatives in Kilmarnock, Inverness and Spean Bridge, and enjoyed family holidays in Troon, Girvan, North Berwick and St Andrews, all of which gave me access to quite a wide area of Scotland.

In April 1966 I bought my first car, a Mini converted and tuned for rally driving, and could now travel long, predictable distances in the day, with the flexibility of being able to choose a strategic spot where I could sleep overnight in the car. By now I was working long hours as a junior doctor, and time was at a premium. Fortunately, with posts in Inverness and Stornoway, I was able to indulge my interest in rural bus operation. However, I had to return to Glasgow to complete my surgical training, and with marriage in 1969 and children coming along in 1971 and 1972, the tempo of my life changed again.

Family holidays with young children gave some opportunity for the photography of buses as well as family. Of these, Carradale, North Berwick, Dornoch, Aviemore, Portree, Inverness and Ireland were all popular British locations with the children. Holiday locum work in Oban, Ballater, Grantown and Castletown added to the variety. In later years, after deregulation, I was making regular visits to my mother in Edinburgh, my daughter in Aberdeen, my aunt in Inverness, and to Kintyre in connection with my work, and the piles of slide boxes mounted up, many of which lie effectively untouched to this day.

However, with the fast approaching elimination of the former Rapson vehicles from the fleet of Stagecoach in the Highlands, this would seem to be a good time to start to look back at the early years of Highland Omnibuses and its assimilation of the MacBrayne bus fleet. The pictures in this book were all taken by myself, except for one from the collection of my friend the late Robert Grieves, who is widely acknowledged to be the finest Scottish transport historian and accompanied me on some of my earlier travels. He had over forty books to his credit, many covering all forms of transport in the Highlands throughout the twentieth century. My book, however, concentrates solely on buses that could be seen in the decade before and the decade after the creation of the Scottish Transport Group in 1969.

Unfortunately, some of the pictures are of poor quality, as I lent all my negatives and most of my slides to a contact in the 1980s. All of the negatives and many of the oldest slides were never returned, and some of the images in the book are reproduced from scans of prints I have managed to retrieve, although I do not now have the original slides. The selection was difficult as the temptation is to show a particular bus as it appears throughout its life, and compare it with the rest of the vehicles in that batch. However, the result is intended to be a brief look at the vehicles, depots and operating territory of the two major bus companies to run services in the Highlands, and also some of the smaller ones. This book, however, just covers the mainland and excludes the islands because, 'The earth belongs unto the Lord and all that it contains, except the Western Islands and they are all MacBraynes.'

The first two Maudslays entered service in 1947 with 1936 Park Royal bodies from rebodied Maudslay Meteors new in 1929. FGB 418, with the body from SB 3362, was rebodied by Duple in July 1958 and is ascending from Corran Ferry to pass DTY 789, a rare Guy with a Meadows engine and Gurney Nutting body converted to full front by Dodds of Troon, as was their custom, now owned by a contractor. The Maudslay was withdrawn in 1967 and later operated for Garner of Bridge of Weir.

Shortly after being acquired in May 1970 with MacBrayne's services operating in Lochaber, HGA 980D, now Highland Omnibuses CD68, one of five 24-seaters fitted with mail compartments, is at Glencoe crossroads on the 8.10 a.m. service from Crianlarich station to Kinlochleven. Connecting with the Glasgow to Fort William rail service, it carried mail north through Glencoe, and was the designated bus for this journey until Kinlochleven depot closed in January 1976.

At its peak, Kinlochleven depot had an allocation of five buses in 1962, with a further two garaged at South Ballachulish. In August 1962, WGG 623, in its original livery with more cream, is waiting to depart for Ballachulish ferry. This was replaced by the bridge in December 1975. Maudslay FUS 994 has come with schoolchildren from Ballachulish village. The mail compartment of 384 FGB, which has just arrived from Crianlarich, is visible, and the other Maudslay GUS 408 is the spare bus.

Above left: Highland Omibuses L11 (NSG 790) was one of twelve Bristol Lodekkas new to Scottish Omnibuses in May 1956 as AA3–14, which were transferred north seven years later at the time of their first MOT. For the next nine years they were the mainstay of the Inverness town services, and on withdrawal six returned to the parent fleet, where they ran for a further four to six years. Parked shortly after arrival at Needlefields, it was sold to Allander Coaches of Milngavie, who kept it for only six months.

Above right: L5 (NSG 784) waits by the South Kessock slipway for the eight-vehicle ferry to complete the half mile crossing of the Beauly Firth from the Black Isle. Until the opening of the Kessock Bridge in 1982, the alternative route was by Beauly and Muir of Ord, so buses from Cromarty and Dingwall connected at North Kessock to provide a more direct service to Inverness. As AA7, NSG 784 operated from Dalkeith depot, but only AA3–5/9/11/4 returned, and operated from Baillieston depot as AA576–81.

It is 2 p.m., and Guy Arab E47 (BST 570), operating from Fortrose depot, has arrived at North Kessock from Rosemarkie to meet E65 (CST 271) from Dingwall. Passengers for Inverness have walked on to the ferry, but today the buses are being changed over, and the crew are chatting before swapping vehicles.The Fortrose decker was normally used only on the school runs to and from the ferry, whereas Dingwall depot, with an allocation of twenty-eight vehicles in 1966, tended to use any available bus.

Above left: Strachans bodied K92 (EST 395), new in May 1951 with thirty coach seats and a six cylinder Gardner engine, and pride of the Highland Transport fleet when it was absorbed in to the new Highland Omibuses nine months later. It spent all but two of its eighteen years in Caithness, where for many years it was the regular vehicle for the Sunday service to Raigmore Hospital in Inverness. Sitting in Farraline Park Bus Station in 1965, it has been rebuilt and downgraded to a service bus with thirty-four seats.

Above right: K89 (EST 393) had a more mundane life, and apart from four years in Caithness operated out of Inverness and latterly Dingwall or its subdepot at Fortrose. Here it is approaching Munlochy, having served the village of Killen on the Saturday-only service from Fortrose, and will duplicate the Cromarty bus to North Kessock. New as a 38-seater, it too had been rebuilt with the loss of beading, but later downseated to thirty-four seats, obtained from Burlingham Seagull bodied Bedfords, in June 1964.

A surprise acquisition in 1965 was K33 (AMS 549), a solitary 35-seat Duple bodied five cylinder Guy Arab single decker from Alexander Midland (MG19), new to David Lawson in 1947, which only ran for six months before being scrapped. Despite the paper sticker for Rosemarkie, it is approaching Munlochy on service from there to North Kessock, to provide connections to Dingwall and Inverness. Although allocated to Inverness depot, it spent most of its life in the flat terrain of the Black Isle.

MacBrayne purchased twenty Bedfords with Duple coach bodies on C class chassis modified for PSV use, but despite the oldest being only twelve years old, only one (WGG 545), based in Harris, was painted in to Highland colours. WGG 633 is parked here at the driver's house near Whitebridge in Strathnairn, where it was the regular bus for a school run from Aberarder to Inverness during 1966 and 1967 before being transferred to Armadale in Skye, and thence to Highland in September 1970.

Highland Omnibuses took over the Achnasheen Hotel Company in March 1965, with connecting services departing from Achnasheen Station at 2 p.m. to the villages of Laide and Diabaig in Wester Ross. Dingwall-based 1947 Bedford OB C9 (FFS 859), rebodied by Burlingham in 1953, was transferred from Scottish Omnibuses (C159) in January 1962. It only had a month left in service before sale to Macrae of Ardelve when it was photographed in July 1965, departing for Torridon and Diabaig.

Timetabled as a mail service, the usual vehicles allocated were MB2 and 3, Kenex bodied BMC microbuses, and in the winter, an 11-seater Land Rover UST 298 which was given fleet number MR1. In May 1967, MB2 (FJS 254), an 11-seater Morris J2 previously with McKenzie of Garve, is parked at the terminus at Lower Diabaig, having completed the last eight miles of unclassified single track road which has come to a dead end. Transferred to Dornoch to work from Lairg, it was withdrawn in 1968.

The Sutherland Transport & Trading Co. operated services which radiated from Lairg Railway Station, and carried mail under contract to the Post Office as well as a wide variety of goods and laundry, which required a large mail compartment. Bedford ANS 571C has a specially built 16-seater body by SMT Sales & Service of Edinburgh, and is parked at Durness having arrived at 5.15 on the three-hour journey from Lairg. New in October 1965, it was six months old when photographed.

SMT purchased a batch of fifty AEC Regals after the war for express services, with Duple bodies which required rebuilding after seven years because of unseasoned timber. Highland Omnibuses acquired eight (B28–9/43–8) in 1962, of which three were allocated to Tain depot when the garage and services of Donald McKay were taken over in October of that year. B43 and B44 carry their fleet numbers in place of route numbers as they wait with K99 to depart on local services in August 1963.

Two buses were garaged nose to tail in the shed at Helmsdale, one for the 8 a.m. service to Dornoch, and the other carried children to Golspie High School. In 1963, both vehicles were Guy single deckers with SMT bodies constructed using Alexander parts at Marine Gardens, on former London Transport G class chassis. K87 (KSC 919) was a 39-seater which entered service in May 1953, and operated from Dornoch depot during 1963, and again in 1965, being withdrawn in December of that year for scrap.

The village of Birichen was provided with a service for shoppers to visit Dornoch every Friday, and church attenders on Sunday, with the services being withdrawn in January 1977 and July 1982 respectively. Willowbrook bodied Ford T72, new in March 1973 in coach livery, had forty-one dual purpose seats and was halfway through its ten-year life when it was photographed traversing the unfinished roads on the circular service, which usually saw 28-seater Bedford VAS CD 4 or CD5.

T63 was still in the blue and grey coach livery when photographed in April 1973 near Edderton on the 11 a.m. service from Inverness to Helmsdale, where it would be parked overnight, having been converted for OMO operation the previous October. It was rebuilt four years later after a major accident, and operated from Wick until sold in January 1983 to MacAulay of Lochboisdale, who operated it in South Uist for many years.

Leyland PD1 J169, with a Samlesbury body built under sub-contract from Leyland, had been new to Wemyss Brothers of Ardersier in 1948, passing to Alexander as RA105 in June 1950, and thence to Highland Omnibuses in February 1952, who kept it until December 1965. Having the underpowered 7.4 litre engine and no platform door, it spent its entire life at Inverness depot, usually on town services or the early Fort George runs, and rarely ventured to Dingwall or Nairn itself.

Waiting in Farraline Park Bus station in Inverness, beside Leyland TD7 J1 and Bristol Lodekka L2, is Guy Arab E51 (BST 571), ready to depart for Holm Mills, a ten minute journey on which any size or type of vehicle could be found. One of eight similar vehicles with Northern Counties bodies (E47/50-2/63-6) purchased in 1946 and 1947, it and E66 were never fitted with platform doors, and E51 remained at Inverness, often on service to Nairn or Dingwall, until withdrawn in December 1965.

AEC Regent D1 (BSD 403), new in July 1947 to Cumnock depot, was a surprise arrival from Western SMT (C440) in January 1963. With its powerful 9.6 litre engine, it had operated intensively out of Inchinnan for the previous eight years, but was not put to good use in Inverness, where it was used principally on the Nairn via Fort George service until withdrawn that November. Painted in to Highland livery, it even had the name substituted in the illuminated strip above the destination box.

Eight years later, Farraline Park is much more colourful following the transfer of the MacBrayne services in the Inverness area to Highland in April 1970. AEC Reliance UGB 697H (BA21) has arrived from Fort William; 44-seater 389 FGB (B58) is about to depart for Fort Augustus, where it is outstationed; and EGA 827C (CD59) for Glenurquhart, where it has been garaged since new. Northern Albion Viking NNV 55E, although screened for Cullen, is only going to Buckie on the 'Coast service'.

AEC Regals KGG 708–10 were new to Fort William in 1953 with 35-seat Roe bodies, and although KGG 708–9 were rebodied by Duple in December 1960 KGG 710, which originally operated the Inverness service, retained its original body, and was transferred to Kinlochleven in 1965 for school duplication. Seen in April 1966, parked near AYS 733B off the Crianlarich mail service, it was withdrawn in December of that year, with KGG 708 and KGG 709 surviving only a further three years.

Maudslay Marathons GUS 930 and GUS 933 were also rebodied with Duple coach bodies to upgrade the service and coach fleet, and GUS 930 is entering the garage in Ballachulish village after arriving back at 7.45 p.m. from Kinlochleven in July 1966. It had left at 7.5 a.m. on a two-hour journey alongside Loch Linnhe and across the Connel Bridge to Oban, where it would connect with the service to Ardrishaig operated by GUS 933. The Connel Bridge had only been opened up to through traffic since June.

The first MacBrayne AEC Reliance to be painted in the recently introduced Highland livery for service buses, peacock blue and poppy red, was WGG 636 in February 1971. Now numbered B50, it has arrived in Kinlochleven from Fort William at 8.50 a.m. on a frosty morning a month later. UGB 428 is still in MacBrayne colours, and has made the short journey from Ballachulish where it is outstationed, before departing again for Oban at 10.5 although it would not leave Oban again until 5.20.

In May 1958, MacBrayne's first AEC Reliance, UGB 428, entered service from Glasgow, but with the opening up of the Connel Bridge in 1966, it was based at Kinlochleven for the through service to Oban, which it operated regularly until withdrawn in December 1975. In May 1970, it had become Highland B43 and is seen here parked outside the office at Kinlochleven depot in August 1973, having arrived from Oban. It had been painted in to Highland fleet colours in December 1972.

AEC Reliance BA31, formerly Scottish Omnibuses ZB120C, with a paper sticker for Oban, is on the through service from Inverness introduced with the opening of the Ballachulish Bridge in December 1975. Connecting with it in the village of Ballachulish at 10.45 in May 1976 is BA21 from Kinlochleven. New shortly before the take over, it was MacBrayne's only short Willowbrook bodied AEC, and spent its entire twelve-year life working in the Fort William area.

Historically, the transport hub in Fort William was at the pier beside the bus station and depot, and the railway station. This historic view from Robert Grieves' collection features GGB 220, one of a batch of four Croft bodied Maudslays which remained at Fort William. Parked on the pier is similarly bodied FGG 635, a 29-seater Commer from a batch of six, of which three had mail compartments. Also parked beside it are Park Royal bodied Maudslays, including GUS 931 with a mail compartment.

GUS 931 was one of a batch of sixteen Maudslay Marathons (GUS 407–12/924–33) bought in 1949, of which the last four were 27-seaters with mail compartments. After GUS 930 and GUS 933 were rebodied, GUS 932 had its compartment removed in 1960 when it was converted to a 35-seater, leaving only GUS 931, photographed here in Fort William garage, which retained its mail compartment until it was withdrawn in May 1962 and sold to Duncan Logan, a contractor in Muir of Ord.

AEC Regal KGG 708 was new in 1953 with a 35-seat Roe body, and was rebodied after only eight years in service, with a Duple coach body. It is waiting at Fort William Bus Station in September 1963 to depart on an afternoon tour. Regularly used to duplicate WGG 636 on the Fort William to Glasgow service, it was transferred to Kinlochleven when the through service to Oban started, and sold in June 1969 to McTavish of Arrochar, who operated it for a further six years on hires and school work.

Two of the 1949 batch of Maudslay Marathons, GUS 411 and GUS 924, had their Park Royal bodies rebuilt by Bennett of Glasgow in 1958 incorporating a full front, and were allocated to Fort William and Kinlochleven respectively. GUS 411 is leaving Inverlochy village, heading into Fort William, in September 1964, but despite being modernised it only survived two years longer than others from that batch, apart from the preserved GUS 926, and was scrapped in March 1965.

Only two AEC Reliances, XGD 775–6, new in August 1959, had Park Royal-Roe 45-seat bodies, which were clearly to BET design, and entered service on Fort William local routes. XGD 775, on a private hire, is followed by Maudslay FGB 418, which is crossing Lochy Bridge on service to Corpach via the village of Caol. The AECs were transferred to Highland Omnibuses with the Fort William area operation in May 1970, numbered B44–5, and B45 remained at Fort William until withdrawn in 1976.

B44 moved south to Oban in February 1972, and for the next fifteen months operated the longer country services, including working from the Bonawe outstation, from where it had arrived when photographed in the town centre with McCaig's Tower in the background. It is about to depart for Ganavan Sands. Reallocated north to Inverness, it spent the next two summers at Aviemore and was sold in May 1976 to Sutherland of Glenbrittle on Skye, who operated it for a further three years.

With the transfer of Alexander Midland's Oban garage and services in October 1970, nine Leyland Tiger Cubs were exchanged for AECs, of which three (GWG 470/4/7) were fifteen-year-old Alexander bodied Monocoaches numbered B72-4. One moved away, B73, transferred to Inverness and also sold to Willie Sutherland two years later, but B74, previously MAC 73 from Crieff depot, remained at Oban until withdrawn in September 1972. It was painted into fleet livery in October 1971.

Four years earlier, after the purchase of the sixteen-vehicle fleet of Norman Smith of Grantown-on-Spey, fifteen-year-old Leyland Royal Tigers, formerly 301/21/5/9/36/41 in the Ribble fleet, were acquired as urgent replacements, becoming J1–6. Initially Highland's Aviemore allocation was scattered throughout the area, with two buses at Carrbridge, one each at Forres and Newtonmore, six at Grantown station where J1, J5 and J6 are parked, and the rest at the Aviemore Centre.

Basic covered accommodation was soon obtained in Grantown, and Bristol LS6G SL9 is about to leave for the 4.5 p.m. service to Elgin via Aberlour in April 1973. New to Western SMT as GT1282 in 1957 at Greenock depot for the Glasgow to Largs service, apart from a year at Stranraer running to Dumfries, it remained there until sold with six others to Highland in January 1972. It was the only one allocated to Aviemore, and the first to be withdrawn after an accident in June 1974.

Highland Omnibuses purchased sixteen Bedford VAS buses and CD27, the first of the 1968 batch, has just been painted in the recently introduced poppy red and grey livery in March 1981. Converted when new for OMO operation, it is leaving Grantown depot for its regular Braes school contract, which requires a small bus, which in the winter is often replaced by a hired Land Rover. This bus spent its entire life at Grantown, being withdrawn when the contract was lost in August 1981.

In the summer of 1975, a second 49-seat Ford in the blue and grey coach livery, T104, was allocated new to Grantown depot for private hire and Wallace Arnold tour work, from which it has returned. To qualify for the government grant of the time, coaches had to operate a percentage of their mileage on service work, and T87 has just arrived at 5.2 p.m. off the 35 service from Elgin, and is due to depart again for Aviemore at 5.35. Two years later, both vehicles were replaced by Duple Dominant coaches.

J3 was the first of the batch to be converted to carry twenty-four sets of skis, appearing from Alexander coachbuilders in November 1967 as a 38-seater. Identifiable by its split destination screen, it has been repainted with cream windows, and is approaching Boat of Garten on service from Forres to Aviemore via Dava moor in May 1970. It operated out of Aviemore and Grantown from entering service in February 1967 until it was withdrawn in August 1971, when it was scrapped.

J5 is leaving the Cairngorm ski park in March 1969 to return to Newtonmore, where it was parked overnight, operating a school service from Laggan in the morning. When it arrived in Inverness via a dealer in Preston, it was converted from a 44 to a 42-seater, fitted for OMO operation, and was initially allocated to Nairn depot for a school run before moving to Aviemore. Despite the later conversion for carrying skis, it was used on all the normal service runs until it was also withdrawn in August 1971.

A variety of vehicles took skiers up to the slopes, including the centre entrance Guy 'bombers' acquired from Western SMT, of which K36 (EAG 472) was in the final batch which arrived in late 1965. New in June 1952 to Western SMT as a 41-seater coach for private hire and duplication on the Glasgow to London service, it was downgraded to service work at Stranraer in 1964, but operated on a variety of services for Highland in Inverness, being withdrawn in December 1969 for scrap.

MacBrayne's first batch of six Thornycrofts in 1948 had Harkness bodies, but only FGE 914 was a 14-seater with no mail compartment, although it was converted in 1951 with only seven seats. Operating latterly on Skye, it was sold to the Craigellachie House Ski School in Aviemore in June 1959, and was still in use when I photographed it in 1965, although the mail compartment had been reduced in size and it now seated ten. It is recorded as last licensed in September 1967.

Former MacBrayne Maudslay GUS 927, the newest of three purchased in October 1962, was still intact when the company was acquired but looks dilapidated, and curiously the fleetname on the side has transposed letters. Although rebuilt without acquiring a full front, it was one of the first of the batch to be withdrawn by MacBrayne. Parked beside it is DRS 666, a rare Alexander bodied Albion FT39N new in 1950 to Simpson of Aberdeen, and identical to CMS 920 at the 1949 show.

Highland reacquired one of a pair of Guy Arab rebuilds, JWS 125, previously K78 allocated to Thurso, and just withdrawn after operating for three years with Smith. However, it was sold for scrap, as was Commer PDA 248, which was given fleet number D5 but taken out of service immediately when it donated its front to D4 (SPT 106), which had a similar Plaxton body. Parked beside them at Needlefields in Inverness is former B45 (ESC 441), an AEC Regal converted to service vehicle H6.

Another unique vehicle to end up with Highland was GSC 457, an AEC Regal new to SMT as their B364 and numbered B36 when it arrived in Inverness. It was exhibited at the 1948 Commercial Motor Show at Earls Court with a new style of Burlingham body which was effectively the forerunner of the Seagull model. With an 8-foot-wide body and thirty-one seats, it proved unsuccessful on the Edinburgh to London service and was soon downgraded to service work and reseated for thirty-five.

Entering service with Highland Omnibuses in March 1962, it proved equally unsuited to urban and rural operation and was detested by the drivers on account of its handling and poor visibility, and by conductresses because of its heavy door. Although allocated to Inverness, it was shunted back and forwards between Dingwall and Dornoch on a daily basis, and sold to Smith of Grantown a year later. Photographed at Newtonmore in April 1964, it had become a store at Grantown by August.

Along with the former Ribble vehicles came Guy Arab UFs with 37-seat Duple Worldmaster coach bodies new to Red and White in 1952. Numbered K44–9, they were immediately allocated to the Aviemore area, primarily for ski and school services, and later converted for OMO operation. K48, parked at Carrbridge Station in June 1967, which arrived like 46 in a cream rather than red livery, has still to achieve fleet colours. Within a year it had moved to Tain, where it ran for a further two years.

The scenic Cairngorm National Park provided opportunities for private hire work, and CD27 is parked near Coylumbridge in 1973, having been repainted from its original red and cream livery two years earlier. Having power operated doors and dual purpose seats it was versatile and, like the other five vehicles in this batch, remained unaltered. However, two of the original 1964 intake, CD1 and 7, were temporarily converted with mail compartments in 1969 for use in Caithness and Wester Ross.

26

Now in fleet livery, K47 is parked in the school square in Portmahomack on a Sunday in May 1970, ready to take the school children in to Tain Academy the following morning. Replaced at Aviemore within months by the Leyland Royal Tigers, all six Guys ended up at Tain depot, where they operated the local and school services, although K44–7 operated briefly out of Nairn garage. Only two of the batch saw further service after withdrawal, K46 and K49 with the contractor William Tawse.

Alexander Northern acquired four Ford and three Bedford six-year-old coaches with Duple 'grant' bodies with the purchase of Simpson of Rosehearty in December 1966. These were quickly passed on to Highland, and two Bedfords are seen parked at Dingwall station in July 1968. CD25 (SSA 474), outstationed at Resolis, has come in from Cromarty via Culbokie, and CD23 (SSA 472) is off service. Both were transferred to Tarbert on Harris in 1970, and sold to Peace of Kirkwall in May 1973.

Nairn bus station was a fairly bleak place in April 1959 when I photographed J161, about to leave for Inverness via Fort George, shortly before it was withdrawn and sold to Hearchar of Beauly for scrap. New to Plymouth Corporation in April 1935, it was sold to Alexander, who rebodied it with an Austerity Alexander body, emerging as R556 in February 1946, and was passed to Highland with the Inverness area services in 1952. It was substantially rebuilt in April 1955 and in daily use until sold.

K81 is sitting at Nairn bus station on Saturday 27 June 1964, about to depart on a private hire, although it would be withdrawn and sold to Kelbie of Turriff for scrap a year later. One of the first batch of twelve 30-foot-long 39-seaters constructed from former London Transport Guy double deckers operated briefly for Scottish Omnibuses (E23–31) or Highland Omnibuses (E87–9), it had operated from Nairn depot since 1960, latterly on a school contract from the village of Cawdor.

Garage space for four single deckers was rented at Knowell and Cummings garage in Nairn, but the double decker for the Nairn via Fort George service had to be parked outside. Ready to leave the depot on tour in July 1965, shortly after arriving from Alexander Midland, is A11, one of two 29-seat Albion Nimbuses which, as MN14 on tour from Stepps depot, had sustained major damage to its Alexander body, resulting in a new front of a different design. Parked beside it is K19, also for tours.

A new depot accommodating ten buses adjacent to the existing bus station was opened in December 1967, and in 1970 former Scottish Omnibuses 49-seat AEC Reliances BA4–7 (EWS 124–6D) were allocated to replace fifteen-year-old 44-seat Guys GL22–5, which were spartan in appearance and comfort. OMO operation had recently been introduced, and the AECs, with the powerful AH590 engine, operated all the services from the depot, and are seen here in the evening in May 1971.

Above left: Highland Transport specified Strachan bodies for its Guy single deckers between 1948 and 1951, but Northern Counties for double deckers. However, its final order to Strachans included an ornate 57-seater double decker with a full front and platform doors, which appeared at the 1950 Motor Show and entered service in March 1951. Becoming Highland Omnibuses E72 a year later, it had to be modified to have a rear emergency exit, and in 1964 was rebuilt, becoming more austere to the eye.

Above right: However, it seemed unstable, was not popular and rarely strayed beyond Dingwall, usually appearing on the Inverness to Nairn via Fort George service, although it was unusual for it to be parked at Nairn depot overnight. Here, it waits there before returning to Inverness at 7.0 on a June evening in 1966. Finally it was dispatched to Thurso at the end of 1967, and made occasional forays to Dounreay reactor site before leaving in April 1970 for Inverness, where it was delicensed for sale.

Finally, it was sold in December to Peace of Kirkwall on Orkney, who required a double decker for a school contract, and joined an ex-Ribble Leyland PD2, ECK 934, which also had a platform door fitted to its Leyland body, a prerequisite for the harsh winter climate. Although this bus returned to the mainland for preservation, E72 was less lucky and after only two years in service was left to rust away at St Margarets Hope, eventually donating its engine to a fishing boat, I believe.

Above left: A surprising arrival in Inverness in January 1964 was J1, a twenty-three-year old Leyland TD7 from Alexander Midland, which as R281 had operated from Milngavie depot most of its life. It was delicensed on 31 December 1963, leaving only one remaining prewar Leyland in service there. Highland had withdrawn J161 nearly five years previously, and PD1 J169 only had two more years in service. Despite being painted, it only ran for four months, being sold to Kelbie of Turriff for scrap.

Above right: Inverness town services had been pioneered by William Greig, who was taken over by Alexander in 1947, and the depot at Carse Road where his buses were garaged passed to Highland Omnibuses in 1952. It continued in use until 1972, when new purpose-built premises were opened in Seafield Road which are still used by Stagecoach today. J1, which had been heavily rebuilt in Alexander's workshops at Brown Street, Camelon, Falkirk, is about to leave Carse Road for the bus station.

Another unusual vehicle arrived in May 1967, this time from Western SMT, who had fitted a 1952 Eastern Coachworks body from a withdrawn Leyland PD1, new in 1949, with a Strachan body requiring replacement, to 1955 PD2 GCS 232 after its Northern Counties body sustained damage. The resultant hybrid, D1146, operated from Cumnock depot for three months before transfer, and as Highland JD6 is seen here at Raigmore Hospital, Inverness. It was scrapped only two years later.

A solitary East Lancs bodied Albion Lowlander was purchased for spares from a dealer in February 1974, in exchange for a Bedford VAS, but proved to be worth overhauling and it entered service as AL45 on Inverness local routes in December, on which it ran reliably for three years. New to Luton Corporation in 1963, 166 EMJ passed through a series of dealers before and after operating for Highland, finally ending back in Barnsley in December 1979.

One of the many Motor Show vehicles to appear in the Highland fleet was HB5 (PWS 998), an Alexander bodied Leyland PD3 with a unique homalloy front, which entered service with Edinburgh Corporation in November 1957 with fleet number 998 on the 19 circular service. It arrived in March 1974 and, being highbridge, was confined to Inverness local services, on which it operated for only two years before sale through the dealer Ensign to Avro Coaches of Corringham in December 1976.

Along with HB5 came five other PD3s, already fifteen years old, with similar bodies but conventional fronts, and HB1–3 are ready to enter service in April 1974. Parked among them are delicensed Park Royal bodied AEC Reliance B16, which had spent nearly all its life in Caithness and never been modified for OMO operation, and another unusual purchase in the shape of a Strachans bodied Ford T11 (NPM 323F) which had recently entered service but proved rather troublesome.

HB1–4 (SWS 261–4) entered service with Edinburgh Corporation Transport in February/March 1959 numbered 261–4 and were renumbered 994–7 in 1971. HB6 (PWS 999) appeared at the same time in an experimental all scarlet livery, but had the same chassis specification as HB5, having a semi automatic rather than manual gearbox. All six were sold to Ensign of Benfleet in October 1976, with only 1 and 6 not seeing further service, and are seen lined up in September before heading south.

Fortrose depot provided vehicles for services on the Black Isle, with four single deckers inside the garage and the double decker parked outside. All were usually Guys in the early 1960s, although when the depot was closed in May 1972, the allocation was three Fords and Albion Lowlander AL22. Nineteen-year-old Guy Arab E47, fitted with a platform door only three years earlier, is parked between shifts on a sunny February afternoon in 1966 only nine months before withdrawal, beside AEC Reliance B32.

Strachan bodied Guy Arab K32 was one of three dual purpose vehicles new in July 1950, all of which retained their original bodies. It was allocated to Dingwall depot most of its life, operating out of Fortrose garage for the last few years, and has stopped outside for a crew changeover while on service from North Kessock to Cromarty in June 1964. It survived another year before being sold to Kelbie of Turriff for scrap. The other two vehicles of that batch, K46 and K70, both ended up with showmen.

K42 was also one of three Strachan bodied Guys, new in 1947 with a more austere looking body, but surprisingly in cream coach livery. It alone remained essentially unaltered, with K41 being rebodied with a second hand Alexander body, and 43 extensively rebuilt in Edinburgh, losing its rear emergency exit. K42, with its 'D' depot plate, is parked at Dingwall Station, about to depart on the Saturday only run to the village of Brahan in September 1962, three months before withdrawal.

A total of forty-one Alexander bodied Guy 'bombers' arrived between 1963 and 1965. K6 was new to Western SMT in 1952 as a 36-seater coach and was fitted with a toilet in 1953, which was removed with the addition of a further five seats before transfer to Highland ten years later. Still in coach livery, it has arrived at Dingwall station at 8.50 a.m. from Muir of Ord in March 1964. Remaining at Dingwall depot, it was painted into bus livery in February 1966 and withdrawn in September 1968.

Dingwall station was busy at 5.0 on a weekday, with buses parked around the war memorial. Northern Counties bodied AEC D1 (BSD 403) is waiting to leave for Tain, similar Guy E51 (BST 571) for Inverness, and E41 (EFS 353) for Strathpeffer. It was new to SMT in 1945 as E18 and came north in 1958. It had a Weymann body, rebuilt around 1950, and again in Inverness in August 1963 when platform doors were fitted, and was the last acquired Guy decker to be withdrawn, in July 1967.

In March 1967, two Northern Counties bodied Leyland PD1s (ND503–4) came from Western SMT, but ran for only five months before being sold for scrap. The first, JD1, is sitting at Tain depot with AEC Regal IV B55, which was especially converted in September 1966 for OMO operation, with a driver-operated folding door. It is operating the Saturday service to Alness via Ardross in July 1967, but three months later turned over on its side near Portmahomack, and was withdrawn for scrap.

36

Mackay's depot at Tain, which Highland acquired in 1962, incorporated two garages. The Peacock blue and poppy red livery had been introduced in 1970, and Dornoch AEC Reliances B19 and 24, now in their third livery, are parked inside the lower shed in the school holidays in April 1974, and would be withdrawn two years later. B19 was the first vehicle painted in this livery in September 1970, which was intended to reflect MacBrayne colours, and initially incorporated the 'Highlander'.

Sitting opposite the garage is Albion Viking AV4, the second of five which arrived from Central SMT (AC1–5) in their blue coach livery when only a year old in 1967. Allocated immediately to Tain depot, it was painted into fleet colours in 1968, and blue and red in 1973, transferred to Thurso in 1975, repainted red and grey in 1978, and withdrawn in April 1981. By now, the former MacBrayne fleet had been redistributed and beside it is AEC Reliance B52 (294 AGE) from Dornoch depot, in for repair.

Highland Transport had always kept at least two buses at Tain, with a double decker on the 7.40 a.m. service to Inverness, returning at 4.0 on weekdays or 7.0 on a Saturday, and providing transport to dances at 'The Strath' on a Friday night. E37, a Guy Arab new in 1946 with a relaxed version of the Strachan wartime body, was the regular in 1964. It had been extensively rebuilt and fitted with a platform door at Edinburgh by Scottish Omnibuses in June 1961, and was scrapped in July 1965.

The other three Guys in the batch E35–6/8 all had platform doors, fitted in 1950 in Greig's body shop, which was retained by them at the rear of the Carse Road garage. They were rebuilt later to a varying extent in Inverness (E35–6) or Edinburgh (E38), and operated in Caithness all their lives. E38, now a 53-seater, has just come down on 25 March 1967 to be delicensed, and is parked at the workshops in Needlefields, where Duple bodied Guy K46 sits, having just been painted into fleet colours.

The first double decker to operate from Tain to the seaboard villages of Portmahomack and Balintore, D3 arrived by chance and was 'hijacked' by the local drivers, who found it very suitable and used it on the morning school run from Portmahomack into Tain Academy. It had arrived in April 1964 from Alexander Midland, and is parked in front of the workshops at Tain beside K77 in June. Withdrawn by the end of September, it ended up converted to living quarters near Durness.

D2–3 were new to Sutherland of Peterhead in June 1945, and were fitted with platform doors. In March 1950 they became Alexander RO683/7 at Peterhead and, surprisingly, moved to Alexander Midland in January 1962 at Kilsyth and Stirling respectively. Their doors were removed, but the enclosed platforms remained, and thus they arrived in Inverness. D2 came in January 1964, but remained there, and was photographed in Laurel Avenue in March, only to be withdrawn at the end of June.

By January 1974 there were two double deckers allocated to Tain depot; BB1–2 were AEC Bridgemasters with Park Royal bodies from Scottish Omnibuses. BB1 (78 BVD) appeared at the Scottish Motor Show in 1961 as Baxter 78, being acquired by SOL in December 1962, and acquiring a Bus Group destination indicator. Moving north in August 1973, it operated initially from Inverness, but was withdrawn in April 1976. BB2 came straight to Tain depot, but survived for only two years.

BB2 was ordered by Baxter, but was delivered direct to Scottish Omnibuses as BB 962 in April 1963, operating from Edinburgh depot until being acquired by Highland, and was also fitted with a triangular destination screen. It is parked here at Portmahomack in April 1974, where it was outstationed for a school run from Balintore to Tain High School. BB1 was also parked in the village for the direct school run to Tain, and on Friday and Saturday nights went to the dance at Nigg.

The third AEC, BB3 was a Renown, new to Scottish Omnibuses as BB963 in December 1963, which also operated from Edinburgh until entering service at Inverness in December 1973. However, it soon moved to Dingwall in February 1974, where it was photographed in April 1975. However, it proved troublesome and was confined to school runs, usually from Muir of Ord to Dingwall Academy, and also withdrawn in April 1976, being sold along with BB2 to Ensign, who eventually scrapped it.

The Bridgemasters were replaced at Tain by Albion Lowlanders AL1–2, which arrived from Western SMT in April 1966 and ran until September 1977. AL2 (TCS 151) also appeared at the Scottish Motor Show in November 1961 as a demonstrator with a preproduction Alexander body. It entered service at Greenock as GN1703 in May 1962, transferring to Newton Mearns in June 1964. AL1 (UCS 601) was the first of twenty Northern Counties bodied Lowlanders for Western, numbered GN 1737.

A second order for the angular Strachan body on Guy chassis consisted of two vehicles which arrived in 1948: K67 (CST 697), which was subsequently rebodied with a second hand Alexander body from a Scottish Omnibuses AEC Regal of the same vintage; and K71, which is about to depart from Dornoch on the connecting service to Helmsdale in October 1961. It had been rebuilt but retained its original emergency exit, and been allocated to Dornoch since the early 1950s, being sold in August 1963.

OMO operation was introduced in Dornoch depot in 1965, but K99, sitting beside the old town jail, still has three months in service before withdrawal in May 1966. A 35-seater with coach seats, it only had a five cylinder Gardner engine, and is about to depart to Golspie for its school run. AEC Reliance B20, now in bus livery, will depart with a conductor for Inverness at 3.55 p.m., but it was not unheard of for centre entrance Guy UFs, or even a rear entrance Guy K57, to operate an OMO shift locally.

The Highland Transport garage at Dornoch was originally constructed to accommodate short vehicles, but in October 1961 seven of the ten buses were full size. C21 was one of six Bedford OBs, new in 1948 with SMT bodies to Duple Vista style, transferred from Scottish Omnibuses in 1957. It was withdrawn a month later and moved north to Shetland. Twenty of the thirty-two vehicles (FFS 856–87) new to SOL were rebodied by Burlingham in 1953 and twelve later came to Highland.

When the MacBrayne fleet was absorbed into Highland, a solitary Bedford SB5 with a Willowbrook 39-seat body was on order, and it arrived in October 1970 as CD75 in the newly introduced red and blue livery. For the next six years it was outstationed at Foyers to operate the narrow lochside route to Inverness, and then transferred to Dornoch in February 1977 for the rural Lairg to Golspie service. Photographed parked outside Dornoch garage, it was based there until withdrawal in April 1981.

When the MST and OST registered Alexander bodied AEC Reliances entered service in 1959 and 1960, they arrived in the present coach livery of cream with red window surrounds and all were later painted into bus livery, and ultimately red and blue. B26, which had been on tours all summer, is parked outside Dornoch garage, about to return to Inverness at 3.55 p.m. 'Kangaroo' K84, from the first batch of 39-seat former London Transport rebuilds, has been at Dornoch since new, and is unfit.

Above left: Albion Vikings AV1–2 (DXA 402/5C) arrived on loan from Fife in December 1966, but did not return until October 1970, when they reappeared at Newburgh depot in Fife fleet livery, retaining their fleet numbers FNV2/5. Parked beside AV2 at Dornoch depot is B40, with the rare style of Alexander body, in the blue and grey coach livery, used on Scotia Tours from Edinburgh with B42. Initially red and cream, it moved to Skye for the Edinburgh service in 1971, and later to Wick as a service bus.

Above right: By May 1970, the 1960 batch of AECs were in bus livery and B24, which was the first Reliance to be formally converted for OMO operation, was now allocated to Dornoch and is parked up on a Sunday with AV2, now also in bus livery. Both buses would depart for Inverness the following morning and return at night, providing they were not redirected in Inverness for other OMO work. The two Fife Vikings had moved north to Dornoch two years previously to replace centre entrance Guys.

Above left: When B55 arrived from Western SMT as CA 932 in 1964, with six other Regal IVs first used on the London service, it was the only 40-seater in coach livery, the others from Cumnock depot being 44-seat conversions in bus livery. It had completed the Sunday Dornoch church run in June 1964, and would return to Inverness the following day, where it ran for a further year before being laid up. Returning to Caithness is E52, unusual because it had a home made rear door fitted in Inverness.

Above right: Ten years later, the Dornoch fleet is all in poppy red and peacock blue, and with an increase to fifteen vehicles, including two ex-Western Lowlanders (AL32/9) acquired in 1971, six buses were parked in open ground nearby. The double deckers operated to Golspie High School, AL32 (AAG 107B) from Brora, and 39 from Helmsdale, where it was outstationed on weekdays. Bristol SL4 (JSD 907), formerly Western DT1271, was allocated to Dornoch on arrival, but is now dilapidated and about to be withdrawn.

Helmsdale was the changeover point for passengers travelling from Caithness to Dornoch and the south, unless a bus was being worked through to Inverness for operational reasons. In 1972 through working was introduced, but on this cold April morning in 1973, Willowbrook bodied Ford T40 from Wick and T44 from Inverness were required to exchange passengers and return to their respective depots. The Fords were fitted with excellent heaters, but were not, however, the most reliable of buses.

Ten years previously, the passengers from Wick to Helmsdale were travelling in Guys and parked at the bus stance in Wick in October 1961 is K41, the rebodied vehicle from the first batch of three Strachans bodied Guys new in 1947. In January 1955, it was fitted with a 1949 Alexander body from a Scottish Omnibuses AEC Regal which had itself been rebodied. It is about to depart on a short working south to Dunbeath, where it is outstationed with E68, which awaits its school run there.

In 1961, Dunbeath garage housed K41 and D121, a Kenex bodied Austin for a school run from Berriedale. Outside sat AEC Reliance B22, for a Dounreay workers' contract, and either E67 or 68, Guy Arabs (ASD 404–5) new to Western SMT in 1943 with Northern Counties bodies. In December 1951, they were rebodied by Eastern Coach Works, and worked out of Carlisle as DY 206–7 until platform doors were fitted in Dumfries and they came to Wick in April 1960, where they ran for five years.

In 1965, Albion Lowlander AL14 was the Double decker at Dunbeath for the 7.50 service to Wick, returning at 6 p.m., with an afternoon school duplicate run. New to Central SMT in June 1963, eight of the batch of ten Alexander bodied Albion Lowlanders came north, and remained in Caithness as AL11–6/8–9 until withdrawn. Seen in July 1966 beside AEC Reliance B2, with Bedford VAS CD1 soon to arrive from Dounreay, it remained allocated to Dunbeath until 1970, and was withdrawn in 1977.

By 1976, there were three regular Wick Fords allocated to Dunbeath, which parked on the open ground beside the derelict garage. T26 (KST 364G), now in current fleet livery, and T40 (MST 40H), still in red and cream, share the service runs. T63 (SST 263K), still in coach livery, and with forty-one dual purpose seats, is the dedicated vehicle to transport staff to the reactor at Dounreay. AEC B31, now in its third and final livery, normally parked at Lybster for Dounreay staff, is at Dunbeath as the driver is off.

Buses departing from Thurso left from a variety of locations in the town centre, and in September 1962, three buses are waiting to depart at 4.0. Guy Arab E38 (BST 326) is leaving for the village of Scrabster, terminating at the ferry pier. K100 (LSC 101) was the last of the six Guys converted from London Transport double deckers fitted with thirty-five coach seats, and about to depart for Wick via Castletown. It was the last to be withdrawn in November 1966. Behind is AEC Reliance B21, for Wick via Halkirk.

Above left: There was also a garage in Mey, where Thurso depot kept two single deckers parked outside, with a double decker nearby on the other side of the road. One of the single deckers was used to take staff to Dounreay, and in June 1964 AEC B14 had returned and was waiting to depart on an evening private hire. One of four Park Royal bodied Reliances new in 1958, it had just been transferred from Inverness and was never fully converted for OMO operation, and was withdrawn in August 1974.

Above right: During the school holidays, a single decker sufficed for the morning commuter run into Thurso, and in April 1973 Bedford VAS CD31 is parked beside 32, the regular bus for the 9.0 'mail' service, which was OMO operated. The third vehicle is similar VAS CD6, the current vehicle on the Dounreay contract. CD31–2 were delivered new to Thurso in March 1968 and operated there until withdrawn in April 1980. CD31 was sold to the Sutherland T&T Co., and CD32 to MacAulay of Lochboisdale.

On arrival from Western SMT in June 1963, E6 came straight up to Thurso, and was the regular double decker kept at Mey until withdrawn in April 1967, when Lowlander AL8 replaced it. In term time it did the 7.50 service to Thurso, returning at 4.10 and 6.0, except Thursdays. Originally London Transport G369 with a Weymann body, it arrived at Kilmarnock in December 1951 and was rebodied by Alexander, reappearing a year later when it was sent down to Lockerbie, operating as DY 1006.

Above left: At different times, the Dounreay contract required different sizes of vehicles, but the aim was always not to allocate one with hard back seats, and Bedford VAS CD6, parked near Mey depot, was the regular coach when seen in October 1971, remaining so until 1973. New to Tain in June 1964, it reached Thurso in 1970, was repainted into poppy red and peacock blue in March 1971, and was stored delicensed at Thurso from May 1977, later reaching MacAulay of Lochboisdale by May 1979.

Above right: B32 was parked in place of AL8 during school holidays in April 1974, and as it had a new engine which needed running in and no suitable small bus was available, it replaced the double decker for the week. AL8 was fitted with a reversing light, and remained on the school run until withdrawn in December 1977. The following year, buses were no longer parked in Mey, being moved to the drivers' houses at Canisbay, Scarfskerry and John o'Groats, from where 53-seat Ford T156 operated the school run.

Along with a solitary Guy Arab came six Daimler CVD6s from Midland in 1965, two 37-seaters with ECW bodies (DA5–6), and four with Burlingham 33-seat coaches already seventeen years old (DA2/4/8–9.) DA2/5–6 entered service in cream and blue, and 8 in bus livery, as shown when it was passing through Muir of Ord on service from Dingwall to Inverness in July 1965, shortly after entering service. All were eventually in fleet bus livery and were withdrawn by February 1967.

The most unlikely service for a full-size, half cab coach not fitted for OMO operation, with a conductor-operated sliding door, high back seats and no boot, to operate would be the mail service from Achnasheen to Gairloch, and along the narrow single track road to the remote community of Laide in Wester Ross, with no conductor. However, Dingwall depot had allocated DA8 in place of the usual CD10 on 23 May 1966, and my girlfriend sits patiently in my car as I photograph it at the 'depot'.

The business of Robertson of Tomich, who operated a connecting service to Beauly via Strathglass, was taken over in August 1967 with two buses. Only UNK 229 was operated and, as C1, was painted into fleet livery in December but sold six months later. A 36-seat Thurgood bodied Bedford SBG, it was new to Gold Star of Elstree in 1955 and ended up as a mobile fish and chip shop. Parked in Beauly in October 1967, it is about to operate the 10.0 mail service back to Cannich and Tomich.

Nine months later, C1 has gone and, as was customary in that era, almost any type of bus could be seen on most Highland routes. GL5 was one of Western's first batch of ten Guy LUFs (KG 1086–95), new in 1954 for the London service, converted to 41-seaters in 1960, all of which came to Highland. DG 1090 ran at Stranraer for two years before coming as GL5 to Dingwall depot in May 1968, and is waiting to depart from Beauly PO at 10.0. In the winter the run was covered by Land Rover MR1.

Above left: MacBrayne's acquired the Inverness to Glenurquhart route in 1936, garaging small buses at Corriemony and Glenurquhart, but on passing to Highland in April 1970, larger buses were kept at the drivers' houses, and T69 is parked at Glenurquhart, soon to do the 9 p.m. Saturday return trip to Inverness in May 1976. New as a 41-seater in coach livery, it had just been repainted into the modified version with a blue roof, but despite this was the regular allocation during 1976 and 1977.

Above right: Another Willowbrook Ford, also new as a coach, T22 is seen parked near Cannich a year earlier, with the inevitable paper destination bill, due to return to Inverness at 1.50. On arrival in June 1969, it was in the standard red and cream colours, but was to receive four more different liveries, despite being relegated to service work within two years. Remaining at Inverness until the last year of its life, it was painted into coach livery in April 1970, and poppy red and peacock blue in October 1972.

In March 1980, T22 then appeared in an experimental livery, which proved unsuccessful, and by August it was in the newly introduced colours of red and grey. In March 1982 it was sold to Berresford of Cheddleton, whose fleet colours were by chance similar. Although not yet allocated to Aviemore, it was on loan when seen at Aviemore station in May 1980, about to depart for Grantown-on-Spey. Still retaining its original coach seats, it had been converted for OMO operation back in 1972.

The Carse Road and Needlefields premises were replaced by a new depot in 1972, and T22 has just been painted into its final livery in August 1980. Parked beside it is one of Aviemore's two ski buses, T74 and 83, which were converted in 1977, with ski comparments at the front of the bus on the nearside, replacing smaller luggage racks with the removal of two seats. T74 passed to Sutherland of Glenbrittle on Skye in May 1983, where the additional luggage space proved useful for walkers.

Above left: T74 was new as a 43-seater in April 1973, operating the 8.15 a.m. 'mail' service from Wick to Helmsdale, moving over to Skye a year later, and to Aviemore after its conversion. It is about to leave the Aviemore Centre in May 1979 on the half-hour journey up to the ski centre at Coire Cas, with steep gradients that only certain classes of vehicles could cope with on a daily basis. Even in its final livery, it was modified to incorporate a broadside advert for the Dalfaber Village complex.

Above right: T83 started life as a 46-seater allocated to Inverness for the local service to Raigmore Estate, but soon appeared on busy long distance routes, especially the Inverness to Fort William service. After November 1977, its history was similar to T74, except that it featured a further two adverts, one for the Post House Hotel in the Centre, and a third one for Haig whisky as seen here, after briefly advertising the Dalfaber Village. Its fate was more banal, as it was broken up in a yard in Carlton, Yorkshire.

CD14, a 36-seat Burlingham Seagull bodied Bedford SBO, was one of only two buses from Smith of Grantown to be painted into fleet colours. It was acquired five years previously from Smith of Turriff. New in 1955, it still appeared in good condition, but went to Sutherland of Glenbrittle after only fifteen months. Although styled as a coach, Highland used it on routine work, and it is due to leave Inverness at 5.35 for Grantown. Beside it is Albion A11, now painted in dual purpose livery.

An unusual purchase in January 1974 was T11, a 1968 Strachans bodied Ford R226 from Irvine of Law, already converted for OMO operation and with fifty-three leather seats. It initially operated from Inverness on longer distance sevices, but had a troublesome one-piece door and was banished to Skye within a year to operate the Ardvasar to Kyleakin service. By May 1977 it had moved to Aviemore, where it ran for three years, and is seen here arriving in Grantown at 8.50 a.m.

The Inverness to Whitebridge service was taken over from Fraser of Gorthleck in 1944 by MacBrayne's, and thus passed to Highland in January 1970. Bedford VAS EGA 833C had come from Skye, and as Highland CD64 regularly operated the service during 1974 and 1975 before being withdrawn in April 1976. Despite carrying mail, it did not have a mail compartment, and is seen approaching Aberarder on the morning return journey from Inverness in August 1974.

The bus allocated to operate on the narrow roads feeding this sparsely populated area on the south shores of Loch Ness was one of Highland's own 27-seater Bedford VAS vehicles, CD29 (GST 502F), new in 1968, which is seen here arriving at Aberarder Post Office the previous year. After only nine years in service, it was sold to MacCuish of Sollas in North Uist. From winter 1975, 41-seater Ford T68, with a similar history to T69, took over and was outstationed at Whitebridge for the next six years.

The original Albion Nimbus, numbered A1, was NSG 869, with a 32-seat SMT body similar to their S1 (LWS 926), which was however of integral construction. It was on loan from Albion Motors from January to June 1956, and when I photographed it at Inverness bus station in April, about to depart on the short run to Beauly, it was my first ever photograph of a bus. It subsequently ran for a variety of operators, ending up with Berresford of Cheddleton, and is now preserved.

Above left: Following this demonstrator, Highland ordered six similar chassis but with Alexander 29-seat coach bodies, primarily for tours along narrow Highland roads, which arrived as A1–6 in the summer. They were not, however, very reliable, soon being downgraded to service buses on infrequent country routes, and A1 and A4 were sold to Smith of Grantown in October 1965. They returned a year later, but only A1 operated again for Highland for a couple of months, the green areas being painted red.

Above right: A1 (KST 50) is sitting at the workshops at Needlefields, where major engineering and bodywork repairs took place, and has just been outshopped in the colours of Willie Sutherland of Carbost on Skye, whom Highland were reluctant to take over. It was the first of many Highland buses, usually one each year, which passed to him for the operation of his unremunerative service from Portree to Portnalong and Glenbrittle. Often, they returned again to Inverness for disposal, as A1 did in 1968.

When new, they arrived in the cream coach livery, but all were subsequently painted in the red bus livery. They had a relatively short life, A5 being the last sold in October 1967 to MacIntyre of Castlebay on Barra. A2–3 ran in Caithness all their lives, but 1 and 4 came from Inverness in 1961. A5 and 6 had operated on rural routes out of Dornoch, but 5 had just arrived in Thurso in June 1964, and was photographed coming down from the depot, heading for Dounreay with a conductress.

Above left: In addition to the daily mail service to Achnasheen, the communities of Wester Ross were served by a two-weekly service to Inverness, which started from the delightfully named village of Mellon Charles. Pioneered by Bain of North Erradale, it passed to Highland in January 1964 with a 1950 Duple bodied Albion LUO 883, which was sent to Caithness as A7. Outstationed at Bettyhill to transport contract workers to Dounreay, it was sold in November 1965 to Webster of Aberchirder.

Above right: Another solitary Albion acquired was A13 (LVD 635), which came with the business of Seaforth MacGregor of Dornoch in May 1967, who only operated school contracts, along with a Bedford and an 11-seater. Five years newer, it lasted less than a year and also ended up with Webster. Shortly to be painted in to fleet livery, it was photographed heading west along the Beauly Firth towards Bogroy on a private hire in October. It then returned to Dornoch briefly until its COF expired.

In the same month six new Alexander bodied Bedford VAMs came for the coach fleet, and were fitted with OMO equipment in the winter for service work to qualify for the government grant. CD16 is descending round the once notorious corner at Berriedale on service from Wick to Dornoch, and back to its home depot at Inverness. Upseated from a 38 to 41-seater, and later repainted into bus livery in 1977, it ended up as a float vehicle at Inverness, and was delicensed in April 1981 for scrap.

The most luxurious coaches at that time, used on extended tours, were still the 1961 and 1962 batches of AEC Reliances with 38-seat coach bodies, delivered in the cream and red coach livery then standard. B39, which with 38 was allocated to Dingwall for this work, was photographed at the east end of Loch Maree in May 1966, returning from Wester Ross to Strathpeffer. Painted into blue coach colours in1971, and red and blue in 1974, it ended up in Caithness, and was withdrawn in late 1977.

A solitary 49-seat Duple bodied Ford, T67 arrived in 1973 for the coach fleet, but was soon cascaded to service work and transferred to Skye. Here it pauses opposite Bedford CD37 near Cluanie on the 9.10 a.m. service from Portree to Inverness. With a new engine, it was being assessed before use on the Glasgow service, but was never reliable; even my children knew its number while on family holidays on Skye. Reseated and repainted red in 1981, it was scrapped after an accident in December 1982.

The first Bristols to come from Western SMT were SL2–3 in June 1971, 38-seat Alexander bodied toilet coaches new in 1966 as KT 2060–1 for the London service. Photographed with the wrong route number near Invergloy in May 1977, on the 9.45 service from Fort William to Inverness and on to Ullapool, SL3 now has forty-nine seats taken out of AV11 and 13, and a grey stripe. It returned to Western in July 1978, becoming DT 2702 operating briefly out of Lockerbie, and was withdrawn in July 1980.

Scottish Omnibuses were never very happy with the batch of fifty-six AEC Reliances new in 1966 because of problems with overheating and, starting in 1969, transferred twenty-two to Highland and six to Alexander Northern. The remaining SOL vehicles were all withdrawn by 1978, the Northern ones in 1980 and the last Highland, BA9, in 1982. At Farraline Park in May 1971, Highland BA5 sits alongside Northern NAC 265 from Aberdeen depot, about to return on the five-hour journey via 'the coast'.

BA1 had just been painted into red and blue when photographed on a private hire near Tomatin in April 1973 before returning to Wick, where it had been allocated since new for contract services to Dounreay. In May 1978 it received the fifty-three bus seats from Ford T148, which was fitted with coach seats to augment the private hire fleet, but they were returned in June 1981 when it was withdrawn. After conversion, it ran from Inverness until it was moved to Nairn for a school contract in October 1979.

Yet another Motor Show exhibit to be operated by Highland was FAG 92, exhibited at Earls Court in 1952, which entered service with Western SMT in May 1953 as KG 1047. It was a Guy UF with a unique 39-seat embellished version of the centre entrance Alexander body, with a sliding door, curved glass roof windows and a revised design of seat. Used for prestigious private hire work, it was transferred to Newton Mearns depot in August, and north to Inverness in July 1965 as Highland K22.

Despite its pedigree, it was treated in the same way as the other similar vehicles, painted in to a variant of the bus livery in June 1966 and reseated with thirty-six replacement seats. Although used on tours, it was primarily a service bus and was delicensed for the winter of 1968. The following May it was relicensed and sent north to Caithness, but lasted only a further year, and I last saw it delicensed in Inverness in August 1970 for scrap. An ignominious end for a fine vehicle – it was never seen again.

Along with E6 came two further former London Transport Utility Guys, HGC 146–7 new in September 1945 as G367–8. Also rebodied in December 1952, they operated as Western DY 1004–5 at Annan and Lockerbie respectively before having platform doors fitted and transferring to Highland. E7 has just arrived at Needlefields on 28 August 1963 and will shortly travel north to Caithness, where all three worked out of Thurso depot. It was the first to be withdrawn in September 1966, and was scrapped in Turriff.

E65 was one of the three postwar Northern Counties bodied Guy Arabs which had doors fitted in the Marine Gardens workshop of Scottish Omnibuses in 1960 when already thirteen years old. Despite this, it remained at Dingwall and never went north to Caithness to transport workers to Dounreay, who in the 1950s demanded that their double deckers had heaters and platform doors. Seen at Needlefields in 1967, it was the last of the batch to be withdrawn, at the end of that year.

The first Northern Counties bodied Guy bought by Highland Transport was AST 957, which became Highland E19. New in 1944 with an austerity body, it had a six cylinder Gardner engine and spent much of its life in Caithness. It was extensively rebuilt and fitted with a platform door in Greig's bodyshop in 1950. Emerging from Wick depot in October 1961 to operate the town service, it ran for a further three years, even on Dounreay contracts, before sale to Hearchar of Beauly for scrap.

Leaving Thurso depot at 7 a.m. three years later is another Northern Counties Guy, with a highbridge body unsuited to Highland's operating territory and confined to local services around Thurso for its year in service. New in March 1946 as London Transport G308, GYL 448 passed to Alexanders seven years later as RO 719 and was refurbished in order to operate Perth's town services.With a heater, but no platform door, E9 appears to have been an opportunistic purchase with a year's 'ticket'.

Inside Thurso depot in 1961, on the pits beside Bedford OB BWG 247, were two of the twenty double deckers operating in Caithness, all Guys with platform doors and the newest fourteen years old. Those on BST 277 (E35) with a Strachans body were fitted by Greig, and on DWS 844 (E33) in Edinburgh in 1959. It was new to SMT in 1944 as E10, with a Northern Counties body extensively rebuilt around 1951. It moved to Highland in July 1958, and operated in Caithness for eight years.

The only other highbridge Guys were also from London Transport, GYL 413/21 (G273/81), which moved to Western in March 1953 as AY 1038–9, operating Ayr local services. They came to Highland in October 1957 as E31/o and were allocated to Thurso, only being fitted with doors, in Inverness, in December 1960. Parked here at Dounreay for the day, they retain their additional illuminated screens. E31 was withdrawn for scrap in September 1964, but 30 survived until October 1966.

In 1963, there were sixty-three buses operating for Highland in Caithness, of which half conveyed staff to the site of the nuclear reactor at Dounreay. They arrived from eight different depots and outstations, and most remained all day, departing as a mass exodus at 5.15 p.m. The Albion Lowlanders did not arrive until 1965, but AEC Monocoaches and Reliances had been sent north when new and usually operated from the more distant locations, such as B11 from Lybster.

Half cab Guy single deckers were still needed to supplement the AECs, and K86 has come from Wick, and K92 on its daily run from John o'Groats. K86 (DST 284) was new to Highland Transport in June 1949, with a Strachans body in cream coach livery with thirty-four high backed seats. Six years later, it was replaced by a 30-seat (increased to thirty-five) Alexander body of the same age from SMT's AEC Regal B394 (GSF 713), which was being rebodied with a Burlingham Seagull body, to augment its coach fleet.

Another unsuitable double decker without a door arrived in Thurso in December 1964, Daimler CVG6 BSD 469 with a 57 seat Alexander body, new to Western in 1951 as KR 957, operating Kilmarnock local services to Hurlford. Numbered D6, it effectively replaced E9 and was not even painted during its year with Highland. Parked beside it at Thurso depot are E32 and 34, formerly SMT E9 and 19. EFS 354 had a Weymann body, also rebuilt by SMT, and was fitted with doors in Inverness.

Four further AEC Regals came from Scottish Omnibuses, this time with Burlingham bodies, and B57, the first of three for Caithness, arrived in January 1965. New in July 1949 as a dual purpose vehicle, and latterly operating at Linlithgow, B371 was in good condition when it came north. Despite this, it only ran for three years before ending up on a farm near Dundee. In July 1965, it has come into Thurso on the mail service from Mey, and, although not suitable, will operate the town service.

In 1976, because of reliability problems, a decision was made to send all the Albion Vikings to Caithness, where operations were less intense, and this included AV8 and 9, acquired with Midland's Oban operation in 1970 as MNV 26 and 71. Parked at Oban in October 1973, AV9, being nominally a coach, is still in blue and grey colours, and AV8 was used on the Glasgow service. Once in Caithness, AV9 was painted into red and blue, but never fitted for OMO, rarely used and withdrawn in late 1980.

All the Vikings were withdrawn by 1981, but were often off the road. Inside Wick depot in October 1978 are AV5 (FGM 103D), rebuilt after a major accident near Oban but now delicensed; 11 (DFS 8C), about to be cannibalised; 13 (DFS 10C), out of use; and 14 (DFS 11C), still on the road. AV11 and 13 had been fitted with forty-four bus seats for operation in Oban in 1973, and 14 had been upseated from thirty-four to forty, but still dual purpose. They were rarely used on Dounreay contracts, and usually on school runs.

Above left: Further Bristol Lodekkas (GM7020–5) arrived at the end of 1969 from Central SMT, who had ordered them with highback seats and platform doors to operate the long Glasgow to Peebles service. As Highland L13–8, they operated for two to three years without ever being painted. L13/6–8 conveyed staff to the Invergordon Smelter, but 14 and 15 came to Caithness. L14 is seen arriving at Castletown on the 8 a.m. service from Wick to Thurso in November 1971, and was withdrawn three months later.

Above right: Three years later at the same location, Leyland Leopard JL5 is going in the opposite direction, with a blank destination screen and meaningless route number. One of four Alexander bodied coaches new in June 1973 for tours and private hires from Inverness, it had been converted for OMO operation and was due to return from Wick to Inverness on a private hire. In January 1978, it moved to Alexander Northern as NPE59, being converted to a 53-seater, operating from Aberdeen depot.

Dunnet of Keiss had operated the service from Wick through to John o'Groats since 1942, with a variety of vehicles. Roe bodied Leyland PS1 AHE 779, new to Yorkshire Traction in 1947, had been acquired in November 1958, and operated the service for eight years. Although very reliable, and powerful enough for a relatively flat road, it had a one-piece opening door and was not very popular. Parked at Wick terminus, it is waiting with its destination set to depart for John o'Groats in July 1966.

Above left: In 1980, ten 79-seat Ailsas (G1–10) came from Fife, where they had entered service five years previously as FRA1–10. All came to Caithness, where they operated until returning to Fife in 1990, later becoming 801–10. G7 (KSF 7N), now renumbered G307, is seen at Greenvale Crossroads on service from John o'Groats to Thurso in 1985, having survived a fire the previous year. G8 was not so lucky and was burnt out in a separate incident. New to Kirkcaldy, it returned to Newburgh until it was withdrawn.

Above right: On Thursdays, Highland operated from John o'Groats to Wick as an extension of the 10 a.m. service from Thurso to Mey, and B21 is seen approaching Castletown in October 1971, with the destination screen set correctly, but the fleet number displayed in place of the route number. Arriving new in cream livery in Caithness in 1959 and outstationed at Lybster to transport staff to Dounreay, it was then in its third livery and confined to school and local services. Three years later it was withdrawn for sale.

Heading in the opposite direction was Dunnet's 36-seat Mulliner bodied Bedford SBG, new to the Royal Navy in 1956 and acquired nine years later, when it was registered ASK 493. One of three similar vehicles, it was used on school contracts and occasionally on the John o'Groats service, when it was photographed near Canisbay. Although it never carried a destination screen, the local passengers knew its route through the myriad of roads serving the local communities en route.

The bleak coastal road from Thurso west to Tongue had been operated by Peter Burr, who converted this Duple Midland bodied Bedford from forty to twenty-eight seats, adding a large mail compartment to transport goods and laundry baskets from hotels. MVD 268, new to Hutchison of Overtown in 1956, passed to Highland with the service in June 1967 as CD26, but was never repainted and was withdrawn for scrap two years later. It was photographed at Reay post office en route for Tongue.

The replacement vehicle for the Tongue mail service was CD13, a further bus operating in the Highland fleet which was exhibited at a motor show. A Bedford VAM with a unique version of the Alexander Y type body incorporating a large mail compartment and twenty-four dual purpose seats, it was photographed at Fort William on 3 June 1966, its second day in service. Destined for Caithness, it first moved to Wick to operate the morning mail service to Helmsdale until CD26 was finally withdrawn from service.

Outstationed at Tongue, CD13 came in to Thurso every weekday at 10.15 a.m. after its two-and-a-half-hour journey via Melvich and Skerray, returning at 1.30. Here it is about to load with parcels at the Highland Omnibuses office, just up from the old bus station, in April 1976, having been painted into red and blue in April 1973. When it was not in service, it was usually replaced by AEC Reliance B13 or Bedford VAS CD1, which had itself been converted with a mail compartment in 1969 as a spare.

The day came for CD13 to be replaced, and on 19 October 1981 it made its last journey to Inverness, with drivers changing vehicles at Bonarbridge as T161 made its way north. CD13 had acquired a more conventional front grille and was in the latest version of the livery, with the grey stripe. T161 was the last of ten 53-seat Fords new in 1977, and had been converted in Inverness with a mail compartment and only thirty-one seats. However, it was withdrawn for scrap only five years later and not replaced.

The first new full size buses to arrive for Highland were six AEC Monocoaches in 1957, with 41-seat Alexander bodies diverted from the Scottish Omnibuses order. B5 is seen sitting at Golspie on a Saturday in July 1968, about to return to Lairg, where it was parked overnight. This service, and the related working from Lairg to Bonarbridge, passed to Highland in 1956 from the Sutherland Transport & Trading Co. as no mail was carried on these services, but the latter run was withdrawn in 1964.

AEC Reliance B19 is passing the depot of the ST&T Co. as it leaves Lairg on the afternoon service to Golspie in March 1966. Being a Friday, it had also run to Bonarbridge after returning from its morning school run to Golspie High School, which most years required a full size vehicle from Dornoch's allocation. However, in school holidays Bedford VAS CD4 or even 11-seater Kenex bodied MB2 sufficed. B19 was the first full sized bus to appear in the red and blue livery, in September 1970.

When all but one of the twenty-six Alexander bodied 44-seat Guy LUFs new to Western in 1955 came to Highland in 1968, GL17–9 were immediately allocated to Dornoch. They remained there until they were withdrawn three years later, but like the rest of the batch they were never painted, and looked increasingly dilapidated. GL19, new as DG 1119 at Stranraer depot, is parked at Lairg on a Sunday in May 1970 for the service to Golspie, but was not withdrawn for scrap for another fifteen months.

Loading up with mail at Lairg Post Office in March 1966 are two of the four Bedfords that would soon depart for the railway station a mile away. After connecting with the northbound and southbound trains, they would deliver mail and goods to many remote Sutherland communities before finally reaching their destinations on the coast. Leaving the railway station at 12.45 p.m., NS 5451 is bound for Bettyhill via Altnaharra and Tongue, and NS 5452 for Lochinver via Rosehall.

NS 5452 has reached Lochinver at 4.30 and is parked for the night. New in February 1964, it has a 16-seat body with a large mail compartment specially built for the company by SMT Sales & Service of Edinburgh, and was one of four constructed on Bedford VAS chassis to the company's requirements, the first, NS 5024, being petrol engined and kept local. NS 5452 and 5451 were withdrawn in 1973 and replaced by Willowbrook bodied Bedfords DNS 354L and 355L respectively.

At Laxford Bridge, the coastal A894 road from Scourie, Badcall Bay and the south meets the A838 road taking traffic from Durness and the north-west coast down to Lairg and the south. This was the meeting point for the bus from Scourie and the connection to Durness, and J series Bedford NS 4745 waits at the strategically placed AA box. New in 1961 with a Duple Midland body with sixteen seats and a mail compartment, it was garaged at Scourie and withdrawn in September 1971 and scrapped.

Six miles further north at Rhiconich, a similar Bedford, 534 BGD, is waiting to return along the tortuous single track B801 road to the fishing village of Kinlochbervie and the terminus at Balchrick. Also parked overnight at Kinlochbervie for a local school contract was an older ex-Highland Omnibuses Bedford OB, either Duple bodied VME 732 or FFS 865, which had been rebodied with a Burlingham 'Baby Seagull' body. It, however, soon passed to Pulford Estates, who transported for the local fishing fleet.

Parked beyond Kinlochbervie at Old Shoremore, looking down over Loch Clash, is a former Sutherland Transport & Trading Co. vehicle now converted into a caravan, which gradually rusted away over many years. An unlikely purchase for the company with its rear entrance, it was a Leyland TS6c, new to Chesterfield Corporation in 1934 with a MCCW 32 seat body, similar to seven which were bought by Walter Alexander & Sons in 1950, and appears to have retained its torque converter.

The school bus kept at Kinlochbervie in May 1966 was VME 732, obtained by Highland Omnibuses in March 1965 when it took over the Achnasheen Hotel Company. A Bedford OB with a 29-seat Duple body, it was new in 1950 to Northern Roadways, who only operated it for four years. Although painted in to Highland Omnibuses livery and numbered C7, it was immediately sold to the ST&T Co., who operated it in these colours and later converted it to a 19-seater with a mail compartment.

Another Bedford OB acquired by Highland Omnibuses was NS 2283, which had been in the fleet of Peter Burr of Tongue since new in September 1949. Also a 29-seater with a Duple body, it had been used on private hire work and a school contract from Tongue to Bettyhill. Although in the fleet at takeover, it was never given a fleet number and never operated by Highland, being sold to a yacht club as a caravan. It was captured at Rhiconich Hotel on a private hire while still with Peter Burr.

The narrow roads of Wester Ross were ideally suited to the Bedford OB, which was still a popular bus for school service and private hires, even in the 1960s, and the Lochcarron Garage operated CRN 440 on such work. The garage still provides transport today, recently operating a school contract from Shieldaig to Gairloch High School, a Monday and Saturday service from Achnasheen to Applecross, and a Tuesday and Thursday service from Kinlochewe to Cuaig.

With the passing of the Bedford OB, there was still a perceived demand for such a vehicle, and in an attempt to revive the concept, Duple brought out the 'Sportsman' body in 1952, with exposed woodwork, using the concept of the estate car. Mounted on a lorry-based Bedford chassis, the OLAZ, the demonstrator MXV 578 passed to MacLennan of Diabaig, who operated it on his service to Torridon and Achnasheen. Now withdrawn, it is still recognisable, parked outside Diabaig in 1968.

M3 joined the Highland fleet with the takeover of the Achnasheen Hotel Company in March 1965, soon being renumbered MB3. It regularly returned to Diabaig to operate the former MacLennan service to Achnasheen station, and had stopped at Torridon post office with mail on its return journey when photographed in May 1966. It was allocated to Dingwall depot, which occasionally provided a different 11-seater for the run, but was sold in June 1968 to Carson of Dunvegan in Skye.

The dedicated vehicle which took over operation of this service was D1, an unusual twelve-year-old 14-seater Karrier with a Strachans body. It arrived as a consequence of Alexander Fife taking over Drysdale of Cupar and had a complex history, with five previous owners. Highland sold it two years later when the Post Office took over in January 1970, and it operated for three more companies. Sitting at Kinlochewe in July 1968, it is waiting for the Gairloch bus to arrive before returning home.

Another rare vehicle was the mail bus that operated from Gairloch along the narrow winding road to the remote villages of North Erradale and Melvaig. John Bain had retained this service and bought Bedford EJS 725 new in 1958. It had a Spurling body with a mail compartment, originally seating eight, but reduced to seven when seen parked at Gairloch in August 1965. With its informative destination screen, it is waiting for the arrival of the Highland bus from Achnasheen before returning home.

Another bus which Highland did not operate was Bedford SB 879 EVK, which was in the fleet of Fred Newton, who was taken over in October 1965. Two months previously, I had come across it at Inverewe Gardens on a private hire. New to Fraser Brothers of Blaydon in 1958 with a 41-seat Plaxton body, it passed to neighbour MacRae of Fortrose, and to Newton in January 1963. Four coaches, three Fords and an Albion, were retained by Highland, but not the two older Bedfords.

Above left: Another bus which Highland kept on the service it previously ran before the operator was taken over was Bedford CD10, yet another demonstrator to enter the Highland fleet. It was new in 1954 with a 26-seat Duple body, but after arriving in Inverness from the Achnasheen Hotel Company in March 1965, it was converted to a 14-seater with a mail compartment before entering service. Sitting at Achnasheen station in July 1968, it awaits the arrival of the train before leaving for Laide.

Above right: July 1965 saw CD10 on the Garve to Ullapool service, as the larger seating capacity Albion normally allocated to this working was required to transport holiday makers to Gairloch during the Glasgow 'Fair Fortnight'. It is parked just round the corner from the post office, ready to depart at 12.10 on the mail service to Braemore and Ullapool. Four years later, it passed to Sutherland of Glenbrittle, who operated it for two years before it returned to Highland and was sent to Kelbie at Turriff for scrap.

On an exceedingly wet day in August 1966, I lay in wait at the east end of Loch Maree for CD10 as it returned from Achnasheen to Gairloch and Laide. Unusually, it had a working destination box, but with a very limited list of places. My car was probably as interesting as the bus, being a standard 1962 Mini which had been fitted with an 1100 engine tuned for rally driving. However, the only clue that it had been tampered with was a straight through exhaust on what was a visibly neglected car.

Above left: Bedford VAS CD30 was new in March 1968, and immediately allocated to Dingwall depot to replace 24-seater Albion A9. It had a Willowbrook body with twenty-seven seats but no mail compartment, and was the regular bus at Ullapool until September 1973, when the service was withdrawn and CD30 was transferred to the Achnasheen to Laide run. When that service ceased in late 1975, it then went to Thurso and was withdrawn in December 1978. It was photographed at Garve post office in July 1968.

Above right: CD12 was an additional Bedford VAS at Dingwall, transferred from Aviemore in 1970 and allocated to Laide. It too had no mail compartment, but a boot was fitted, and it is seen at Achnasheen station in August 1970, waiting to load up with the mail which has come off the Inverness to Kyle of Lochalsh train. Now in its third livery, it moved on to Dornoch in 1973 and was withdrawn four years later. It then moved west again to Clan Coaches at Kyle, and later to Lewis with Kennedy at Orinsay.

One of the sixteen Bedford VAS buses bought new, however, did appear in a unique livery, which was not to last long. CD8, from the first batch, also worked on the network of services in Wester Ross, but not the mail contracts. There were shoppers' buses to Inverness, and a weekly service from Gairloch to Ullapool, operated light from Dingwall. It is seen sitting at Inverness, waiting to depart on the Thursday-only service to Laide, in July 1966 but was withdrawn after a crash near Ullapool in November 1968.

Above left: Albion A9 joined the Highland fleet when MacKenzie of Garve was acquired in October 1964, and it too continued to operate the same service as before the takeover: the mail service from Garve station to Ullapool. New in 1955 with a 32-seat Strachans body, like CD10 it too was converted with a mail compartment and the seating capacity reduced to twenty-four. It is parked along from Achnasheen Station in this photograph taken in July 1965, as it had been swapped round with CD10 for capacity.

Above right: The extensive mail compartment in A9 is clearly necessary as it loads up at Achnasheen Station before departing at 1.0 for Gairloch and Laide. However, conventional coaches were occasionally used and T7, a nine-year-old 41-seat Plaxton Ford, was regularly substituted in the summer of 1973 in place of the smaller Bedford VAS. Half cab Daimler DA8 appears in an earlier picture, but centre entrance Guy UFs K11 and 12 regularly appeared on the Garve to Ullapool service when A9 was off.

Most of the passengers and mail are destined for Gairloch and A9 has just arrived, two hours after leaving Achnasheen, much of the journey being among spectacular scenery along the shores of Loch Maree. It then continues up the beautiful coastal road to Poolewe and Aultbea, terminating at Laide over an hour later. A9 only lasted until June 1968, when its COF expired, and it sat at Highland's workshops at Needlefields in Inverness for some months, later turning up in Northern Ireland.

Further south, the Ardnamurchan peninsula provides equally stunning and dramatic views, and MacBrayne's Bedford VAS 386 FGB and C5 609 CYS are waiting at Ardgour Ferry to head west to the villages of Acharacle and Kilchoan respectively in August 1962. The VAS was new in May, with a mail compartment and twenty-one seats for this service, later altered to only twelve seats. Highland restored it to a 28-seater service bus (CD49) in 1971, and sold it two years later to Lochs of Crossbost on Lewis.

Above left: Highland Omnibuses took over MacBrayne's Lochaber operation in May 1970, and allocated a similar Bedford VAS, 848 HUS, now Highland CD52, to the Acharacle outstation. It had started life in 1963 with only twelve seats and an extra large mail compartment to operate the mail service which connected with the train at Kingussie, leaving at 4 a.m. for Fort William. Later reduced to only eight seats, Highland converted it to a 24-seater, and it is parked near the ferry at Ardgour in March 1971.

Above right: CD52 was the first Bedford from the MacBrayne fleet to be painted, and in August 1970 it appeared in an experimental red and cream livery. CD53 followed, but this was not adopted, and the red and blue colours were favoured instead. In May 1971, MacDonald of Kinlochmoidart took over operation of the two services and CD52 moved north to Thurso to act as a spare mail bus for the service from Tongue. However, mail buses were not now in favour, and it was withdrawn only a year later.

Above left: Kilchoan was the furthest west point on the Scottish mainland to be served by MacBrayne, and in August 1966 Bedford VAS HGA 980D, only three months old, is returning from Acharacle, having connected with the bus from the Ardgour ferry at Salen. The journey time was two and a half hours over very rough roads, and in the summer it continued right to the ferry to provide extra capacity. Although this was the regular bus, Highland handed over an older mail bus, 384 FGB, to MacDonald.

Above right: HGA 980D became Highland CD68 in May 1970, and was painted into the standard blue and red livery two years later. It had moved to Kinlochleven and, unusually, survived in service with its mail compartment until January 1976, when the depot closed. Parked near the driver's house in Ballachulish on a Sunday in August 1973, it will depart on the 6.15 a.m. mail service from Kinlochleven the following morning. Only HGA 983D remained in service longer with its mail compartment.

Another service which Highland gave up was the local service from Mallaig to Arisaig, which passed to Morar Motors in July 1976. As part of the MacBrayne network, it was disconnected from the main Fort William operation, but a bus was parked overnight near Mallaig station. In August 1966, 28-seater Bedford VAS AYS 734B was the regular vehicle and it was photographed near Arisaig, passing the famed silver sands of Morar. As Highland CD55 it moved to Skye, but was withdrawn in 1972.

Glenelg was another MacBrayne terminus near the end of a single track road, and HGA 982D is parked up for the night, having traversed the hilly road over from Ratagan and Loch Duich. The service starts at Kyle of Lochalsh, connecting with the train arriving from Inverness, and was taken over by Highland Omnibuses in September 1970. However, it passed to Davidson of Glenelg in July 1971 and HGA 982D, now Highland CD70, moved to Skye as a spare mail bus, remaining until 1974.

Above left: The most spectacular feature on this service was Eilean Donan castle, and HGA 982D has crossed over the bridge from Dornie, heading for Kyle of Lochalsh. It was one of five 24-seaters with mail compartments new in 1966, each allocated to a particular mail service. Of the others, three operated on islands: HGA 981D on Skye for the Kilmaluag to Portree service; HGA 983D on Islay for the Port Ellen/Port Askaig runs; and HGA 984D on Skye at Dunvegan for service to Kyleakin.

Above left: HGA 982D was the only one of that batch to lose its mail compartment with Highland Omnibuses, and in January 1972 it was converted to a 28-seater and painted in fleet colours. It then replaced HGA 981D at Kilmaluag, which had joined a pool of unwanted mail buses, moving to Dornoch in 1975. By then, it was frequently off the road, and was photographed at Tain depot waiting attention in July 1976. Withdrawn at the end of the year, it ended up back on Skye with McLeod of Dunvegan.

There were two Willowbrook bodied AECs with forty-nine seats in the MacBrayne fleet which passed to Highland and later ran on Skye in coach colours. BA20 came from Inverness in 1973 to operate the weekly Uig to Edinburgh service, and is seen driving onto the ferry at Kyle of Lochalsh to cross over to Kyleakin in July 1974, returning north. Painted in bus livery in 1975, with a manually operated door it was not suitable for local work, and was banished to Thurso in 1976 and withdrawn in June 1981. It is now preserved and appears regularly at events all over the country

The first batch of new small vehicles to be bought after the influx of twenty-two Bedford OLAZ vehicles in 1952 were thirteen C class Bedfords seven years later. Seven were 28-seat buses, and WGG 625 is still painted in the original cream version of the livery when photographed on the pier at Kyleakin in April 1962. It remained on Skye until transferred over to Tarbert on Harris for the Maruig school run in 1967, staying until Highland acquired the operation. It then returned to Skye with Sutherland of Carbost.

Kyleakin pier was the terminus of MacBrayne services from Portree, Ardvasar and Dunvegan which awaited the arrival of the train at Kyle of Lochalsh from Inverness at 2.30. In August 1966, HGA 978D and 984D were only three months old. The former was about to depart for Portree and the latter, which had a mail compartment, for Dunvegan via Sligachan. Both passed to Highland in September 1970 with the Skye operation, becoming CD67 and 71, and were withdrawn in 1977 and 1974.

Six years later, and CD71 from Dunvegan now connects at Sligachan and no longer runs down to Kyleakin. Waiting on the pier is one of two Bedford SB5s new to MacBrayne in August 1969 with 40-seat Willowbrook bodies, UGB 138H, now Highland CD41, which has arrived as a duplicate from Portree. The service bus is Bedford VAS EGA 829C, now CD61, which had moved to Skye from the Inverness operation. Both vehicles are now in the livery adopted after the takeover of MacBrayne.

CD41 (UGB 138H) had been purchased by MacBrayne for the Glendale to Portree service taken over from Carson of Dunvegan, along with similar CD89 (UGB 137H) for the Craignure to Tobermory service. When the Mull operation passed to Bowman of Craignure in April 1976, CD89 also came to Skye, and both buses remained on the island until they were withdrawn in 1981. When seen at Drumnadrochit in August 1971, CD41 is returning from Inverness to Portree in service, after attention in the workshops.

The later livery used on the C class Bedfords eliminated the extensive area of cream, and WGG 621 was seven years old when photographed in July 1966 with driver Sandy MacDonald at Fort Augustus. It was parked overnight for the 7.50 service to Fort William the following morning, while Bedford VAS AYS 737B went north to Inverness. WGG 621 passed to Highland as C1 in May 1970, but like the rest of the batch was not operated, and was immediately sold to St Mary's School in Greenock.

Although most of the coaches used on private hire and tours were necessarily of restricted size, five Bedford SBGs with Duple Vega bodies were purchased new; 41-seater SGE 427, new in 1957, which had moved up from Glasgow to Skye in 1966 is seen sitting on the pier at Mallaig. Two of the earlier batch, with thirty-six seats, had five removed to provide luggage space for passengers with ferry connections on Skye and Mull, but SGE 427 was rarely used on service work and was sold in 1969.

The Bedford VAS with 29-seat Duple Bella Vista body was the mainstay of the coach fleet used on extended tours, and 372 FGB is seen sitting on Oban pier in 1964. One of eight coaches new in 1962, it passed to Highland with the Inverness operation in April 1970 as CD42, continued on private hire work, and was sold to Bowman of Craignure on Mull six years later. Three of the batch were sold by MacBrayne as early as 1968; two more went to Highland, and two to Midland, who sold them on.

The quintessential MacBrayne service bus for island operation was the Bedford OLAZ, derived from a lorry chassis, with a Duple Sportsman body. KGE 243 was the last of the order, fitted with a mail compartment and only fourteen seats. Parked outside the post office at Kyle of Lochalsh in September 1964, it is deputising for the regular bus, KGD 908, on the mail service to Glenelg. It had spent most of its life on Islay, latterly at Port Ellen as a spare bus for private hires and tours, and was sold in 1966.

KGD 901 was a 20-seater mail bus when new, but over the years it was progressively reduced to thirteen, then nine and finally only eight seats in 1964, due to its use on the Kingussie mail service. Finally, in 1966, the inevitable happened and all the seats were removed so that it became a van, still based at Fort William and joined by KGD 906, also converted. It was photographed at the railway terminus by the pier at Kyle of Lochalsh in July 1968, and was sold in May 1970, passing to the Invernesshire Scouts.

The MacBrayne service from Kyle of Lochalsh to Inverness was a single journey, only running on Saturdays, and also Tuesdays in the summer. Nevertheless, a bus was parked at Kyle of Lochalsh at the north end of the village all week for this run. Bedford OLAZ KGB 262 was the regular vehicle until VAS 377 FGB arrived in May 1962, and it was parked in the usual location when seen in September 1963. Later replaced by older coach bodied YYS 176, it moved to South Uist and later to Highland.

Parked outside the MacBrayne depot in Oban in May 1963 is Maudslay GUS 930, which has arrived on service from Ardrishaig, a journey of forty miles taking two hours because of the tortuous bends on the hilly, narrow road. A similar vehicle, GUS 933, is operating the opposing service from Oban to Ardrishaig. The cream area on the side was soon painted red. Both vehicles were new in 1949 with Park Royal coach bodies and were rebodied by Duple in June 1959, but only survived until 1968 before being sold.

Left: The railway branch line between Connel Ferry Station and Ballachulish opened in 1903, providing a connection between the slate quarries and the Oban to Glasgow freight trains. In March 1966 this was closed, and for the first time traffic could cross Connel Bridge without being held up when a train crossed. In August 1966, the railway track had not yet been lifted when rebodied AEC Regal KGG 709 was crossing on the recently introduced through service from Kinlochleven to Oban.

Below: Even with the railway track removed, there was still a requirement for traffic control on the Connel Bridge, allowing ex-MacBrayne AEC Reliance B60, now allocated to Kinlochleven depot, to cross on its return journey from Oban in October 1973. The service was interworked with the Oban to Ardrishaig run, requiring five vehicles, with three based in Ballachulish. New in 1962, B60 had operated in Lochaber all its life and was sold to a dealer in Carlton for scrap in May 1977.

Above: Another of the 1962 Bedfords with Duple Bella Vista bodies to pass to Highland was 376 FGB, which became CD44 when it was transferred with the Lochaber operation in May 1970. It transferred to Mull, where it worked for the next two summers, being painted into coach colours in December 1971. In September 1973, after a season at Oban, it was photographed crossing Connel Bridge on a contract, despite the Skye destination. It was sold in January 1977 to MacDonald of Acharacle.

Below: This was an unexpected vehicle to see crossing the Connel Bridge – an ex-MacBrayne bus in Western SMT livery. However, EGA 834C had been new in 1965 to Ardrishaig depot, although it was often at Lochgoilhead for the connecting service to the Rest and Be Thankful. It passed to Western with the Ardrishaig operation in October 1970, being numbered E3, and has come up to Oban on service and has operated a school run north to Barcaldine before returning to Ardrishaig at 5.0.

The last two Duple Midland bodied AECs to arrive in the Highland fleet, 388 FGB and 392 FGB, came with the MacBrayne operation in Oban in October 1970, were numbered B65 and B66, and curiously were painted into coach livery. B65 remained at Oban, and was photographed in the bus park in April 1971, just after being painted. Kept for tours, it was withdrawn in April 1976 after an accident. B66 went to Thurso, and was used on Dounreay contracts before sale to a local farmer in 1977.

After the Oban operation of Alexander Midland passed to Highland in October 1970, and the Leyland Tiger Cubs had been exchanged for AECs, parked in Oban garage in July 1971 was B80, formerly MAC 205 at Stepps depot, still in Midland livery and unfit. Against the wall was B72, previously MAC 66 at Crieff depot, now in fleet colours, and B43 from Ballachulish on a changeover on the service to Oban. It too has still to be painted into red and blue and adds to the variety of colours.

On the streets of Oban there is also variety, with two former MacBrayne vehicles in their new liveries. HGA 985D was new in 1966 and also allocated to Ardrishaig for the service to Oban. Passing to Western in October 1970, it was numbered E2 and continued to operate this service, alternating with E3 until 1976. It is due to depart at 5.15 on 19 June 1972, surprisingly with a conductor, having collected passengers off AEC WGG 635, now Highland B49, which has just arrived from Kinlochleven.

Down at Ardrishaig, parked at the pier, is the Highland contribution to the Oban to Ardrishaig service, an Alexander bodied AEC Reliance B79, previously Midland MAC 204 at Stepps depot, which will return at 1.15. Beside it is former MacBrayne Bedford KGD 904, which was kept at Port Charlotte on Islay for hires and the church run. With a low mileage and a mail compartment, it was a good buy for its new owner, McLachlan, who was still running it to Tayvallich in July 1973. It is now preserved.

Still recognisable as an Alexander body, with the destination layout of buses in the Alexander fleet, Nairn Bus Station is the final resting place for WG 1122. It was new in 1932 as a dual purpose vehicle for Walter Alexander & Sons as P133, a Leyland TS4 with a 32-seat front entrance coach body. Transferring to the newly created Highland Omnibuses in February 1952, it was numbered H170 and was withdrawn the following year. It was still intact when photographed in February 1966.

Highland Transport bought a couple of AEC Demonstrators, a double decker HX 1388 in 1931, and a single decker MV 1878 in 1932. It became Highland B54 in 1952, but was sold in 1954 to Hearchar of Beauly, who used it in his fairground. It had been rebodied with the 1937 Cowieson body off Gilford HSG ST 9465, rebuilt and converted to front entrance by Highland, with its original body ending up as a store on a farm in Culloden. It was photographed at Beauly in April 1964 with former Guy K42.